MAKE
THEIR
DAY

THE POWER TO MAKE GUESTS

HAPPY

MAKE THEIR DAY

THE POWER TO MAKE GUESTS

HAPPY

CHARLES GREMILLION

The Culture Guy at Embassy Suites Hotels®

Make Their Day:
The Power to Make Guests Happy

Written in collaboration with Miles Page of Tribe, Inc.
Published by Tribe, Inc.
Atlanta, Georgia

Manufactured in the U.S.A

ISBN 978-0-9819803-2-4

With appreciation
for every single person who ever gave me a chance,
and with even deeper gratitude to the Embassy Suites team members
who serve our guests with passion.

CONTENTS

PREFACE

At Embassy Suites, we believe we can do anything. We're humble, but at the same time we believe Embassy provides best-in-class service. We're the brand that allows people to be themselves and to use their own personal strengths to elevate our service experience to a higher level. And we want people to have fun in the process. That spirit is a direct reflection of our culture.

I equate culture to the core of a golf ball. A golf ball is made up of the cover, which is what you typically think of when you picture a golf ball. But underneath that cover is a strong core. Without the core, it wouldn't matter how powerful your swing was or how perfect your form – the ball wouldn't go anywhere.

At Embassy, our culture is that core. Building a strong culture is essentially creating that core. Ultimately, everyone can rally around that culture and express it in their own individual ways. When that happens, when you take actions to put a strong and meaningful core in place, you can move faster and more effectively as an organization.

I was honored when Charles asked me to write the Preface for this book. Inside, he's managed to capture the essence of what makes Embassy so special. It comes from a genuine understanding that when team members are happy, when they find meaning and fulfillment in their work, they're able to step up and tackle any challenge that comes their way.

For us, that culture is called **Make a Difference**. And since we introduced that platform three years ago – with the input and feedback from team members at every hotel – it has grown stronger every year.

One area that Charles and I both like to focus on is recognition and the effect that it can have on an organization. In fact, one of the central concepts of **Make a Difference** is the power of peer recognition. For me, the real power lies in telling others how they have *made a difference* for you. When you do that, it not only makes the person on the other end feel great; that positive energy carries over to you. It reenergizes you and makes you more passionate about going out and helping others.

In this book, Charles has managed to condense 20+ years of hospitality experience into just twelve chapters. Whether you have a lifetime of experience in hospitality or this is your first time working in this industry, if you truly take to heart Charles' teachings on leadership and engagement, you're sure to find long-term success. And after reading this book, you'll likely feel as if you've known Charles for years.

Shawn McAteer
Vice President, Brand Performance Support

INTRODUCTION

Although our business is built on teamwork, those teams are made up of thousands and thousands of individuals across the Embassy Suites brand. The success or failure of Embassy Suites is in the hands of each one of those individuals as they engage in the many gestures, small and large, which add up to any guest's experience with us. One person – every person – has the power to mess it up or make it great, one interaction at a time.

It's up to the people managers and other leaders in our organization to coach our team members on the many ways they can make a guest's day. How? That's what this book is all about.

I decided to write this book because culture is something that I'm truly passionate about. It's what I wake up in the morning thinking about. And I'm grateful that part of my job is to find new ways to help give team members the support they need to be their best. But as you'll see in the following chapters, that's something we all have the power to do.

I grew up in the hospitality industry, starting as a reservationist. From there I moved into sales, and eventually switched over to the management track. I've seen firsthand the opportunities for career growth that our industry has to offer.

When I joined the Embassy Suites/Hilton family, I knew that I'd found a great match. Our **Make a Difference** culture – which encourages every team member to be gracious, engaging and caring – is at the core of Embassy Suites. But while some people see culture as one of the "softer" skills in business, it's actually the magic ingredient that separates truly great businesses from the rest of the pack.

And at the heart of culture are the people behind the brand. The people who are the face of Embassy Suites to our guests. In hospitality, that face might be the smiling person who greets you at the door, the responsive engineer who has a solution for every problem, or the dedicated housekeeper who never compromises the quality of her work. Culture is that thread that ties tens of thousands of individuals together under a single mission.

Effective culture, though, isn't something you can push on people – and it's not something that's easy to change. It takes a focused effort, consistency and time. Team members have to embrace culture, and more importantly embody it, in everything they do. If a company can reach that level, wonderful things start to happen. You'll see people working in an environment of trust, honesty, integrity and transparency. You'll see teamwork and innovation on a whole new level. And you'll also find a business with a competitive advantage that might not show up on a balance sheet or in a company's annual report: A truly motivated workforce. A workforce that operates at a high level day in and day out and finds satisfaction in solving business problems, identifying new opportunities and delivering on the brand's promise.

Today, as Embassy Suites' Director of Brand Culture and Internal Communications, I find myself in the unique position of having an insider's view of the culture at Embassy Suites. And it never ceases to amaze me how far our team members will go to create an excellent experience for our guests.

Culture is something that covers a number of related business topics: leadership, employee engagement, talent, recognition and communication. As you read, I hope that you'll see how culture weaves through each of these different areas. A company's culture is organic and evolving, but its values stay the same. Employee engagement, brand essence, customer loyalty – all tie back to a brand's promise, which is ultimately a reflection of that company's unique culture and way of doing business.

So whether culture is something that is near and dear to your heart, or it's something in which you've taken a newfound interest, I hope you'll see some of the many different ways that we can all *make a difference* while growing as individuals – and growing as a business.

People Manager Help Sheet
Want to talk to your people about culture?
There's a downloadable worksheet to make that conversation easier. Simply visit the ES Make a Difference site and select the Resources tab. Under Materials, you'll find a link for Make Their Day. Each chapter has its own activity that you can work through with your team.

CHAPTER 1
THE SECRET

THE SECRET

The thing nobody talks about in the service industry is that it's an incredible high to know you've made someone's day. We're accustomed to thinking about what it feels like for those on the receiving end of any kind word or heroic deed. But what about how it feels to be the one doing the giving?

Think about the last time you did something really nice for someone. It felt great, right? That's what we want happening at all our properties every day. We want each of our team members to experience the fantastic feeling of making guests happy – over and over and over. Even if the money is great and the benefits fantastic, people are happier when they genuinely enjoy the 40+ hours a week they spend on the job and find fulfillment in the work that they do.

Companies that truly make this connection – no matter the industry – are very likely to find success. Why? Because the team members are the heart of any company.

It's hard to buy top talent – and expensive

Let's imagine a hypothetical company. The company seeks out the most talented people in the industry. It starts by hiring its competitors' top talent and paying them well. These new team members enter the business motivated to make an impact in their area of expertise. For years, the company does well.

It outperforms most of its competitors. But that's when the problems start to show.

This new pool of talent doesn't have much allegiance to any organization. They're constantly looking for the next job. Eventually, this hypothetical company doesn't have enough open positions to meet the demands of a workforce that is constantly looking out for their own personal interests, rather than wanting to grow with an organization.

Where do they look for those new opportunities? Wherever they can find them, quickly moving on to their next jobs.

Now let's take a moment to consider a company with a more employee-centric culture. This company gives team members the support they need to be successful. Employees enjoy their work, and it shows in their customer service scores. People are happy, and rather than looking for new opportunities for advancement outside of the company, they tend to stay on board – growing with a company that promotes from within.

When new team members are hired, they quickly learn the culture from their colleagues, many of whom bring decades of experience and knowledge to the table. They also learn the culture from the tools and resources available to them. The organization is built on a strong foundation. It focuses on creating a nurturing atmosphere that helps people grow. It's not arrogant, but it could be – and over time, the business is growing. Yet what we find is a humble culture that is always looking to deliver a quality service and be thought of as a good organization with which to do business.

Why? It all comes back to culture. And this culture encourages employees to internalize the brand values and express them in their own individual ways. A funny thing starts to happen. Rather than having to be someone that they're not, team members find the opportunity to be more of who they are. They're empowered to bring their own skills to the table, and it creates a rewarding environment.

A Culture of Service

In many ways, culture is really just another way of saying "service." Building culture means elevating the service experience. And the strongest cultures deliver a better, more consistent experience.

It all comes back around full circle. A better experience leads to happier customers. Happier customers become repeat customers who spend more. And serving happier customers is rewarding to team members, who in turn continue to deliver a better customer experience. But that experience has to be consistent, time and time again. If the person at the front-desk sets the tone for a wonderful stay, everyone else has to follow through and deliver that same level of service. And that experience has to be consistent across the brand.

So why don't more companies focus on culture?

I think the smartest companies do. But today's business climate is often focused on short-term results. Falling short of analyst expectations can represent billions of dollars in lost value for large companies. And culture is still somewhat of an abstract thought. It can be difficult to measure and demonstrate a clear ROI for a culture or employee engagement program. Yet culture, as we've mentioned, is one of the most important factors affecting job satisfaction, recruiting and retention, and employee morale.

This gap leaves many team members feeling that something is missing from their work. Maybe the company's values are always changing. Maybe leadership says one thing but does another. The result is a lack of open and honest communication. Without transparency, you can't have trust. Employees are left with a job, not a rewarding and growing career.

So what's the secret to culture? True employee engagement. And it can't spring from selfish or insincere reasons. That's to say that a company shouldn't approach the problem by thinking, "We need to make our business stronger, so we need to invest in our culture." Instead, that company's leadership should think:

- What can we do to provide our team members with the support they need to be successful?
- How can we allow our team members to do what they do best?
- How can we empower team members to use their individual talents and skill sets to better serve our customers?

In this book, we'll discuss building a stronger culture and creating an environment where team members thrive. Because at its heart, a strong culture is about doing right by people. And when people truly buy in to that culture, it creates an incredible ripple effect that reaches everyone who comes into contact with that organization.

It means that the bar is set even higher. That people believe they can achieve more. Culture creates an atmosphere that people want to be part of. It's rewarding and it provides people with an opportunity to grow. It's a magical combination that has a lasting effect on any organization. And while leadership plays an important role in communicating and oftentimes defining that culture, it means nothing if it's not carried out by team members.

CHAPTER 2
THE POWER OF THE INDIVIDUAL

THE POWER OF THE INDIVIDUAL

Every team member in our entire organization needs to understand the incredible power they hold. Every guest services manager, every engineer, every bartender, every housekeeper holds tremendous power to make or break a guest experience. That's why it's so important that we find ways to spread the passion of our culture throughout the ranks, as well as the pride in the guest experience we're able to provide, one human interaction at a time.

So how can we elevate ourselves and *make a difference* in the process? It all comes back to The Power of the Individual. Every team member has the power to *make a difference*.

We each have:
- The power to smile
- The power to help
- The power to lead
- The power to teach
- The power to make their day

Now, let's look at some of the ways we can all *make a difference*.

The power to smile

The routine flexing of the facial muscles on either side of your mouth is so simple anyone can do it – but its power can be immeasurable. A smile tells the person on the receiving end that they are welcomed, they are important and they are among friends. Some of us can't communicate those things even with 1,000 words.

Imagine you're a business traveler who caught a 5 a.m. flight, landed three hours later, collected your luggage, took a taxi to a conference center, gave a presentation, sat through a conference call and downloaded some financial data you have to analyze before you go to sleep. You're a walking concoction of tired, jet lagged, overworked and stressed – all topped off with a bit of crankiness.

But when you reach your hotel, the gentleman who helps you with your bags and opens the door is smiling. The woman at the front desk who checks you in is also smiling. So is the bartender offering you a glass of wine at the Evening Manager's Reception. And the young woman on your floor delivering extra towels to the room two doors down. It's the whole cycle of hospitality, carried out by each individual participant.

Unless you just had the mother of all disastrous business trips, those smiles are going to start smoothing your rough edges. Even for the traveler who doesn't want a lot of interaction and just wants to get into their room, a smile says it all. It's about relying on your intuition to deliver the experience that each guest is looking for.

The beauty of smiling is that anyone can do it. You have to be trained to work the computer check-in system. You have to know what you're doing to maintain the swimming pool in each hotel. And it takes some culinary skills to stay one step ahead when the breakfast rush hits. But smiling is a "skill" we all have; it is the language we all speak. So don't forget that the most powerful asset we have at our disposal is that powerful muscle that creates a smile. And don't forget to share those smiles with your team, too.

The power to help

We all have the power to help those around us. While we each work in our own specific job roles, that doesn't mean that's all we can do. Because we're all working towards the same goal: to take care of our guests and exceed their expectations.

One way to lend a helping hand is simply to ask where you can offer assistance. While we all carry the burden of delivering a great guest experience, sometimes the weight of that task isn't distributed evenly among the team. A moment of relief for you very likely means someone else on the team is very busy. So keep an eye out for little ways you can help.

But sometimes, the best way to help is to rely on our own intuition. If we see something that needs to be done, we each have the power to tackle that challenge. And sometimes, we can find ways to help in the most unexpected places. For example, Kenny Russell, a Shuttle Driver for Embassy Suites Columbus – Airport, gave his advice on ways to help:

"We can all find ways to help out. It's just about taking the initiative. Go outside of what you normally do. In Columbus, Ohio, we get a good amount of snow. This can make it difficult for guests. Not only are they here when the snow comes down, but they don't have the resources to get to their cars. I make sure to clear off everyone's car before they even notice that they were covered. It is not a part of my job, but I do it anyways."

At your hotel, there are countless "hidden" ways to help. You just have to look around to find them.

The power to lead

Leadership isn't something that's just for a company's executives. In fact, it has nothing to do with your job title. Leadership is something that plays out at all levels. And when we take a closer look, it's amazing how many "unsung heroes" are out there leading the way.

Leadership doesn't have to mean that you're in charge of managing a group of people. It's taking a sense of ownership over what you can control and inspiring those around you. I like to say that the 'E' in our Embassy Suites logo stands for "everybody does everything" – and that includes leadership.

By being a leader, by being a good steward of what you are responsible for, you are able to elevate the stature of the organization. You're able to elevate the stature of your team, and most importantly, you're able to elevate yourself. Leadership doesn't stop with you – you're where it begins.

So how can we make that leap? By building relationships. By

asking those around us what's important and meaningful to them and helping them get there. Just as we teach our team members to do whatever it takes to serve our guests and exceed their expectations, the best leaders extend that same hospitality to their teams.

The Selfless Leader

True leaders know that their success depends on the success of their teams. They're able to rally their teams around a cause, to give people the confidence and encouragement they need to tackle new challenges with enthusiasm. Anyone who adopts that mind frame is already far along the path to becoming a leader.

The power to teach

Whether you've spent your whole career with Hilton Worldwide or you've only been here a few weeks, we all have valuable knowledge that we can pass along to our fellow team members, especially those who are new to the team.

In this business, no one comes right out of school and starts as the GM of their own hotel. People start at the bottom and work their way up, learning the ropes along the way. Mentorship is something that is built into that process. During my time at Embassy, I've worked under a number of great people who've taken the time to help me identify my natural talents and shape my career path. They gave me a chance by thinking of me not as who I was at the time but as who I could become.

So next time you see someone new to our team struggling with a new task, offer a helpful tip and use your own experience to help them get the hang of things.

The power to Make Their Day

The power to smile. The power to help. The power to lead. The power to teach. They all lead up to the power to make their day. The power to *make a difference* – for our guests, for our team members and for ourselves. By taking ownership over our roles and inspiring those around us, we see the many different ways that we each can make an impact.

Now imagine the power that comes from harnessing our talents and focusing all of that energy on serving our guests and supporting our teams. And judging from the countless stories I've heard of team members going above and beyond in ways both large and small, many of us have already embraced this entrepreneurial spirit.

CHAPTER 3
THE IMPORTANCE
OF THE TEAM

THE IMPORTANCE OF THE TEAM

Individuals come together to form teams, and those teams are what make our business go round, day in and day out. The more each individual can give of his or herself to the group, the more they continue to grow as individuals. But the team also allows each individual to be a human being, with both strengths and weaknesses, good days and bad. By helping each other out and backing each other up, our teams become a safety net that elevates the guest experience.

In our jobs, each of us is asked to be a team player. We're expected to bring a high level of commitment to our work. We're taught to support our team members, to trust one another, to look for ways we can lend a hand to any team member who needs it. We often say that the person we help today may be the person we rely on tomorrow. This devotion to team is so much a part of our culture that it's almost second nature to us.

On the other hand, we're also encouraged to be genuine and authentic at work and to let our individual personalities show in the way we interact with guests and each other.

How can we be a team player and still be fully ourselves? The irony is that by being part of something bigger, you don't lose yourself. In fact, you're more likely to find yourself. Being a committed member of a strong team provides an opportunity to discover more about who you are and who you can become.

Think of the members of a band or orchestra. They are harmonious in their performance, creating music that is much more satisfying to hear than any one instrument on its own. They are all playing the same piece of music, each musician supporting the others, every player working together to bring the composition to life.

At the same time, each musician must play his or her own instrument. The drums are as different from the guitar as the piano is from the flute. Only by letting their individual instruments be heard are they able to create the powerful sound of their collective music. By giving their best to their individual performances, they're helping the entire group excel.

That's how it is with us at Embassy Suites because we truly believe in *making a difference*. We're asked to give the best of ourselves, to truly be ourselves, at work. We're also expected to give our best to our team. If we do both, we'll find that each amplifies the other. So the better we play our own instruments, the greater the performance of our team. And the more we give of ourselves to our team, the more we become the best version of ourselves we can be.

But no matter how much we say it, if we want team members to truly embrace our culture and be themselves, they have to see the bigger picture. The challenge is that they can't do it by themselves if their managers don't support them and set the example. They have to internalize the idea that they are part of a much bigger operation and that their contribution is not isolated.

As a brand, we are each in charge of carrying out our promise to every guest who walks through our doors. Whether you're in housekeeping, sales, food and beverage or any other group, most team members first see themselves as part of their own department. And while we each take pride in our "first team," communication and respect between departments will help our business grow. And I love to see a healthy competition when different departments are striving to be the best - because in the end, the guest wins.

At the same time, we're all part of the Embassy team. Guests don't differentiate people based on their job role, and they should feel that they can reach out to anybody in our hotels for whatever they need. So while you can have pride by department – and that's a good thing because your department is where you are building your skill set – to the guest we are all the same. That's because we each have equal power to shape the guest experience.

But the team doesn't end with Embassy. While we should all take pride in everything we do inside of our individual hotels, keep in mind that we're all part of the larger Hilton Worldwide family. We're part of a world-class organization, and the potential for advancement is as big as the universe. Your world doesn't end at the more than 200 hotels bearing the Embassy Suites name. It extends to over 1,200 hotels around the world that are part of the Hilton Worldwide global enterprise, a number that is growing every month.

Team members have to see the big picture

So what can our people managers do to help their teams grow? A good people manager not only looks for particular traits that will make his or her team stronger but actively seeks out individuals who have those qualities. They say that the smartest thing you can do is hire somebody who is smarter than you and whose strengths complement your team's weaknesses. If you start with that foundation and explain the bigger picture, you can nurture the relationship through recognition – an incredibly powerful force.

At Embassy, there are countless ways to give recognition freely. In our daily huddles, for instance, we have the opportunity to share other team members' successes. Another way team members can give recognition is by passing the Medallion. As it goes from team member to team member, it keeps those pats on the back going in a circle.

We also have Catch Me at My Best, which is an easy way to recognize someone who you see going above and beyond. Anyone can give a Catch Me at My Best card, and if you haven't seen one in a while, it might be time to give a few out. Finally, there's Spirit of Pride, our top honor and a lifetime achievement award.

Spirit of Pride

Joseph Hughes Jr., a Front Office/Valet Attendant with Embassy Suites Buffalo, was nominated for the Spirit of Pride award for his devotion to his team and our guests. In his nomination, Joe's team described him as having "an amazing personality that complements our vision of 'Be Hospitable.'"

For instance, one Sunday morning – which happens to be his hotel's busiest checkout day of the week – Joe arrived for his 6 a.m. shift. He quickly discovered that the kitchen was in a jam because of a broken dishwasher. Joe immediately took action, doing dishes for two hours, without anyone asking him to, before jumping over to handle the valet rush.

Helping another department while expecting nothing in return, all because it seemed like the right thing to do.
That's the Spirit of Pride.

By giving recognition freely and encouraging others on our team to do the same, we can elevate the team by elevating the individuals who work so hard to make our organization a success.

CHAPTER 4
EMBASSY'S FORMULA
FOR SUCCESS:
BEING GRACIOUS, ENGAGING AND CARING

CHAPTER 4
EMBASSY'S FORMULA FOR SUCCESS:
BEING GRACIOUS, ENGAGING AND CARING

At Embassy Suites, our formula for success is simple: to be gracious, engaging and caring. It's something that we encourage each of our team members to do. The beauty of this approach is that each individual participant has the power to carry it out in his or her own unique way.

One of our most important tasks in getting new team members up to speed is helping them absorb this aspect of our culture. If they can make that link in their own minds – that being gracious to others, for instance, is not something that costs them a lot of effort but something that makes their own days better as well – then the rest of the training is just logistics.

For most people here at Embassy, that sort of behavior is second nature. It's so engrained in our interactions with guests, as well as in the ways we work with our fellow team members, that we may not need to make a big deal about explaining this approach to new recruits.

In fact, I'd go so far as to say that we communicate this part of our culture most powerfully by what we do rather than what we say. We can say over and over again that our goal is to *make a difference*. But no matter how many times we say it, a real-life demonstration leaves a more lasting impression. When new team members see us go out of our way to help one of our colleagues, when they notice the little things we do for guests that sometimes make such a big difference, they get it. Soon they too begin looking for ways they can *make a difference*. Being gracious, engaging and caring is the foundation of our culture.

Being gracious

Gracious is the first word of our Service Statement, and it's the first step towards making our guests feel important, valued and appreciated. Imagine the hostess at a party, the father of the bride or your mother at Thanksgiving dinner. Being gracious means being attentive, thoughtful and kind – all the things that define hospitality. When we show graciousness, we make others feel welcomed, cared for and special.

As you go about your week, be mindful of the times when you see those around you being gracious. You might be surprised when you realize that you don't have to look far to find examples happening every single day.

Doyle Hurt is gracious

Like many of our team members, being gracious is all in a day's work for Doyle Hurt of Embassy Suites Minneapolis – Brooklyn Center. From shoveling snow during a winter storm to helping repair a guest's glasses, Doyle is always looking for ways to help our guests and his fellow team members. And all the while, he does it with a smile on his face.

Being engaging

Being engaging means making a true connection with others. To make our guests feel valued and welcomed, we must provide them with a meaningful experience while in our care. We should never make them feel like they are simply customers but instead like they are guests in our own homes – the way we would treat cherished friends.

So how can we be engaging? One way is to truly listen to what the other person is saying. All too often, people carry on conversations waiting for their turn to talk rather than truly listening to what the other person has to say.

But perhaps the easiest way to be engaging is simply to be the first to smile and say, "Hello." That small gesture could be the catalyst that completely changes a person's outlook on their entire day. And, the warmth that comes back to you feels amazing.

Vince Campagna is engaging

If you don't see Vince Campagna when you walk into the Embassy Suites St. Louis-St. Charles/Hotel & Spa, you might want to check the **Make a Difference** board, the hotel's Safety Team or the **Make a Difference** Committee.

That's because being engaging is something that comes naturally to Vince. Recently, he went out of his way to make a lasting impression on an Italian couple who were staying in his hotel after their house had flooded. Besides making them feel at home by conversing with them in fluent Italian, Vince also left during his lunch break to buy fresh bread to serve with a homemade lasagna he'd prepared for them. And although the couple was dealing with the hassles of a flooded home, Vince was a bright spot in their day.

Being caring

The hospitality industry is a people business. It involves serving and caring for others as if they were guests in your own home. In order to be successful in this industry, you have to sincerely like people and enjoy making them happy.

We all know what being caring looks like, but it can be a bit harder to define. At its heart, being caring means having great and sincere concern for others. It can even mean being protective, looking out for other people.

When guests spend their time and money with us, they are also entrusting us with their well-being. We're responsible not only for their comfort, but for their safety and security as well. It's a great responsibility and a true privilege.

Kelvin Parker is caring

Kelvin shows the true spirit of hospitality in everything that he does. And although anyone he works with at Embassy Suites Cleveland – Downtown would describe him as gracious and engaging, being caring is where Kelvin truly shines. For example, when Kelvin discovered a lost wallet in his hotel, he took it upon himself to find the rightful owner. He started by searching the hotel's computer system, but couldn't find any rooms under that name. So he turned to the internet, found a few phone numbers and called to leave messages. The young woman's father called Kelvin, thanking him for the effort, and Kelvin was able to return the wallet completely intact before she even knew she'd lost it.

By being gracious, engaging and caring, we can all
Make a Difference

The truth is, not everyone can be all three every single time and all at the same time. But we can demonstrate all three by focusing on the traits that come naturally to us. For instance, I'm not always good at being engaging because I'm somewhat of an introvert. But I'm much better at being gracious, so I try to go out of my way to remember what's important to people, to say thank you and to show people that I care. So although engaging can be tough for me on its own, I can be engaging through being gracious and caring. It's a fine balance that's unique to every individual.

Each one of us is encouraged to be our authentic selves. That alone saves so much energy that would otherwise be wasted trying to seem like people we're not. It's much easier to be engaging with guests, not to mention your team members, when you're able to relax and be yourself.

As Embassy Suites continues to grow, this is one piece of our culture I believe to be incredibly important to safeguard and cultivate. As we all go through our days, I invite each one of us to look for even more ways we can model this behavior and to reinforce the efforts of others we notice doing the same.

As you go through the week, take time to stop and think about the task that you are doing. It may be as simple as straightening a lampshade or picking up a piece of paper someone may have discarded. Does this small gesture contribute to the overall guest experience? Of course it does. Even seemingly small actions like these prove that you take pride in your work and have embraced out culture of being gracious, engaging and caring.

°

CHAPTER 5
THE FIRST KEY TO ENGAGEMENT:
BE YOURSELF

THE FIRST KEY TO ENGAGEMENT:
BE YOURSELF

One of the most important things we ask of our team members is that they be authentic. Because one of the strengths of our brand is the world of different experiences and personalities that our team members bring to work every day. Embassy Suites is a place where guests can be themselves, where kids can run through the lobby in wet bathing suits, where a business person can relax and have a drink after work at the bar. There's no reason any of our team members need to pretend to be something they're not.

It starts with the first orientation, when we talk with team members about empowerment and our 100% Satisfaction Guarantee. Any team member is empowered to make a guest happy. If a guest comes to us with a problem or concern, no matter what our individual job title might be, we are in a position to *make a difference* and make things right. We don't have to ask our supervisor or general manager what to do because we are each empowered – and entrusted – to take control of the situation. When people first join the Embassy family, they quickly learn that we all wear more than one hat. And over time, it becomes second nature to stretch ourselves to better serve our guests.

So how can we be ourselves?

The first question I'd ask is, what makes you, *you*? What unique skills and experiences do you bring to work with you every day? For some of us, it might be that we are fluent in another language. If so, it oftentimes allows us to connect with our guests on a more personal level and create a true environment of hospitality. Or maybe it's something entirely different, something less tangible. Eagerness, kindness and integrity are all just as powerful, even if they seem more subtle. Because what makes you, *you* is what lets you react and respond to whatever comes your way.

It would at first glance seem easier if we simply followed a script when we came into work. We'd just learn the correct response to every situation and then do it. But in that environment, no one has a chance to shine.

That's because being yourself comes from within the individual who expresses it, whether that's a housekeeper saying good morning on an elevator or the front desk person checking you in. Instead of a simple acknowledgement, we might instead ask, "How was your flight?" or, "How may I help you this morning?" All of that just comes from inside, and it starts with you.

I've been in other hotels where I felt that the managers didn't really want to hear other people's opinions or even value their contributions. I truly believe that in Embassy, that's exactly the opposite. Our hotels are very relaxed, and we can't function well without people's spontaneous and voluntary contributions of themselves. It may not be unique to Embassy, but it's something we do quite well.

That's because Embassy can't be its best if we're not our best. And part of being our best means growing in new areas, focusing on our strengths. Usually, it starts in your own department with an appreciation for the fact that your job title does not define you or limit what you can achieve.

For instance, if I'm a sales manager and I'm in charge of tour groups, I'm never going to learn the corporate market side of the business unless I make myself available to help and to learn. But once I have a good grasp on my own department, I can take the next step of communicating with and learning from other departments. The more we understand and appreciate that connection between departments, the more we are able to understand the bigger picture of Embassy.

When we're ourselves, it encourages guests to open up and be themselves

As I said, we're the kind of brand where guests can be themselves. We pride ourselves on being a relaxed brand where our guests have the space and convenience to put their feet up. We're not a buttoned up, suit-and-tie type of place. We strive to create a relaxed environment, and when our team members are relaxed, it helps the guests to feel that way too. When everyone is being themselves, it fosters an environment where we can make real human connections.

As a team member, we're less concerned with saying or doing the right thing because it just comes naturally. It becomes a human-to-human interaction rather than a transaction.

DoubleTree by Hilton is focused on the ideal of returning humanity to travel. In short, they recognize that we can be completely dehumanized as travelers by the time we make it to the hotel. We've been through security screenings and treated like cattle as we make our way to our destinations. The idea of hospitality is to return an element of humanity to this individual standing in front of you. To be warm, inviting and appreciative. And I'm still amazed by the positive response and change you can see in people when you warmly greet them. It's often the element that they've been missing all day. That all comes from simply being ourselves. When you bring something of yourself, you open yourself up to the guests and your fellow team members on a whole new level.

Being yourself can build confidence

It all ties back to the idea of being part of the team. It's providing you a safe environment and the support you need. From nine to five, seven to three, three to eleven or eleven to three, we become one another's extended family.

A huddle to remember

The inspiration for Embassy's huddles started with some of our sister brands in the Hilton family. But even before we made the huddle the status quo at Embassy, many of our hotels took it upon themselves to start doing daily huddles in their own hotels.

For example, the owners of the Embassy Suites Fort Worth – Downtown noticed that their team members were often late coming to work and would grab a quick "breakfast" from the vending machines. Because in the rush to get their families out the door in the mornings, they themselves didn't have time to eat breakfast.

So they started these huddles and offered their team a complimentary breakfast every morning, simply by cooking more eggs. They set up a buffet in the break room and invited every team member to come in early for a bite to eat before work. They used it as an opportunity to engage with people. It was like a light bulb went off, and people started to open up to one another. Even the shyest person has the opportunity to share something about themselves.

Suddenly people start to grow a little bit and perk up a little bit, but even better, they bring that great attitude out onto the floor. The first guest they run into in that elevator will be blown away by the warm greeting.

Compare that experience to someone feeling rushed in the morning. Your husband's irritated because he can't find his keys. You're throwing clothes on your kids in a hurry to catch the bus. The second you arrive, you rush to your stand up meeting, grab your cart and race to the elevator thinking about how many rooms you have to clean. A guest asks for more towels, and you're still feeling rushed because you haven't settled in yet. It's hard if not impossible to make a genuine human interaction with a guest when you've had that type of morning.

So the huddle started as a way to nurture people in the most basic sense and get them off to a good start for the day ahead. People were able to leave any negative energy behind and come out of their shell before ever seeing a guest because they knew they were in a fun, safe and warm environment.

As people managers, one of the things we can do is talk with our team members about their individual approaches to being gracious, engaging and caring. Which one of those values resonates most with each of them? How do they see themselves bringing those values to life in their interactions with guests?

To start, we have to let our guard down and show our teams that we're only human too. Like our team members, we're still learning new things each and every day. It's acting less like a boss and more like a mentor. Obviously, a boss has boss things they have to do, like planning and scheduling. But in the day-to-day function of the job, the more you're doing the work with your team and alongside them, the more respect you're going to have and the more appreciation you'll be able to show. It works both ways. The manager is going to grow through that experience, too.

Remember: Whatever makes you, *you* is a good thing. Each of us possesses unique natural talents that make us who we are. When we are able to find opportunities to use these talents at work, then we are perfecting these talents as skills that benefit the brand. The brand benefits from inspired individuals who feel empowered to create a wonderful guest experience by harnessing the power of what's inside of them to make things happen - to *make a difference*. The better we are as individuals, the better our team is, and the better the brand is, which means we all have more opportunities to learn and grow, as people and as a business. This is a continuous cycle that always brings us full circle back to you, the individual.

CHAPTER 6
THE SECOND KEY
TO ENGAGEMENT:
STEP UP

51

CHAPTER 6
THE SECOND KEY TO ENGAGEMENT:
STEP UP

One of the things I love about the Embassy Suites culture is the likelihood that team members will choose to step up and do things that aren't part of their job descriptions. When we teach people to take personal responsibility for the guest experience, they often go far beyond what you would expect ordinary hotel employees to do.

For instance, recently some guests in our hotel in St. Louis went out to a restaurant in the neighborhood and ended up with a flat tire. They didn't know anyone in town, so they called the hotel for help – and they got it. Two of our team members jumped in a car, drove to the scene, changed the flat tire for the spare and then arranged for the dealership to come to the hotel to take a look at the car.

That's part of what makes Embassy so special. Team members at all levels are always looking for new ways to step up. And in the process, they often find more engagement – and a lot more meaning – in their work.

Much like recognition, "stepping up" doesn't have to mean a grand gesture. In fact, stepping up is often expressed most powerfully through the smaller things that might go unnoticed if we only did them once. But when people in your hotel see you doing those small gestures time and time again, they start to take notice. I love to see when a team member comes into work and immediately pitches in and starts helping out, even without being asked. Even as little as five minutes of your time when you arrive in the morning helping out at breakfast can make a world of difference. Picking up a tray and taking it to the bus station, pouring coffee to stop the bottleneck at the coffee machine, showing our guests to a table as they arrive. It can be as simple as being out in the lobby before we get buried away at our desks or in the back of house. Some of those actions take as little as ten or fifteen seconds, but they set the tone for the entire day.

As we start to step up and give more of ourselves, it organically creates engagement in the process. It really is as simple as that. We get to know new people on our team that we might not have had the chance to meet otherwise. We find new ways to give recognition and appreciation. And almost always, we start to find out that other people will have our backs when we need a helping hand. All of that positive energy springs from stepping up.

Stepping up: The Embassy Suites Way

Have you ever been to Neiman Marcus®? What about The Ritz Carlton®? In my experience, both of those places offer a world-class experience. For those brands, it's all about white glove professionalism. In some ways, it's almost the ultimate kind of service.

But at Embassy, we do things a little differently. It's a more informal professionalism. We're here to help you, but not to smother you. We're not all over you as your taxi arrives, grabbing your bags in anticipation of a quick tip. In fact, many of our guests want just the opposite. They're seasoned travelers who know what they're doing. They want to wheel their bags in and check in quickly, they want to know that we're here to help if they need anything, and they want to be treated with respect. When we deliver on those fronts with a smile on our faces, we've won.

Of course, that's not to say that all of our guests fall into that camp. Some people want to be pampered as much as possible. That's where you step in. You have to show a little intuition and shape the guest experience for everyone who walks through our doors, whatever their needs might be. It's something that takes practice, but it's a lot like learning to ride a bicycle – once you learn it, it usually sticks with you. It's true hospitality.

But truth be told, no matter how much experience we have, sometimes our guests will ask for things that we as individuals can't deliver. For example, I'm confident in most guest-facing situations. But if a guest stopped me in the hallway and told me that their television wasn't working, they'd be hard pressed to find someone who knew less about the inner working of TVs.

The secret, though, is that that's okay. But whoever a guest stops with a problem needs to be responsible for finding the solution. So I can say right away that I will have an engineer come by and take a look. But now's my chance to step up. I could follow up 30 minutes later to make sure the problem's been resolved. Or if I'm about to leave for the day, maybe I could just let the front desk know to check on the nice young couple with the twin daughters and make sure their television is up and running. It's about taking ownership of the situation, even if you're not the one who can provide the immediate solution.

In a lot of ways, stepping up simply means anticipating a need before it's expressed. It's hospitality in its truest form. It means being proactive, being the first person to hold out your hand. It's greeting someone first. Being the first to open a door. Asking a guest in the morning if you can bring them a cup of coffee.

That's the thing: If you wait for a guest to ask for something that you could have already noticed, it's not really hospitality anymore. Instead, it becomes more of a simple business transaction than a genuine human interaction.

You might be thinking to yourself, "If I spend all of this time and energy focusing on all of the small things, I'll never get my job done." To that I'd say it's all about frame of mind, and the two aren't mutually exclusive. The job is something that is always happening. It's how you approach that job that makes all the difference. And over time, as we become more confident and experienced, the two simply become one in the same.

How can you step up?

The idea of stepping up is something that is very dear to me because I've seen firsthand the impact that it can have. My first job out of college was working at the reservations office for a big convention hotel. We had tons of corporate clients and group reservations, and it might not be too much of a stretch to say that one of the only reasons I got the job was that I could type. The hours were long and the pay was far from glamorous, but I enjoyed it. After a little while, people started asking for me by name simply because I was friendly, I remembered their names, I knew their corporate codes by heart and I had memorized what their rates were supposed to be.

Even that simple gesture is a form of stepping up, and it leads to engagement in the process. By doing that, I found myself doing a lot more than just my job. Simply typing and answering the phone might have seemed like enough, but it would have meant treating every guest like a stranger. So the more I grew in that role, the more other people in the hotel started to take notice. My boss noticed because she was getting comments, which led her to ask me what else I would like to do in the hotel. From there I moved into sales – an area in which I had no real experience – and launched my career in the process.

When we step up, our guests step up, too

When we step up and treat our guests with genuine respect, they often start to open up to us. It's a little bit of a give and take. We give enough that our guests can let their guard down and be themselves. Any act of kindness is reciprocated. Being human takes down some of those barriers, and it really is the thing that makes Embassy so special. At The Ritz Carlton, I think you're more likely to find that type of guest that simply wants the red carpet rolled out for them and to be treated like royalty. And they should have that expectation. It's that brand's promise.

But for us, it's a little different. Many of our guests who are business travelers find themselves hundreds of miles away from their families. They've just had a long day of meetings and conference calls. So when we step up, are kind and show them true hospitality, it provides something that's been missing from that person's day. They're able to put some of that stress behind them.

The more that we're able to give our guests the freedom to choose what they want – even if it's as simple as choosing between bacon and mushrooms in their morning omelet – the more of an impact we can have on the business. As I've said before, the stronger our culture, the stronger our business. And that starts one relationship at a time.

CHAPTER 7
THE THIRD KEY TO ENGAGEMENT:
WE ALL DO IT ALL

THE THIRD KEY TO ENGAGEMENT:
WE ALL DO IT ALL

Just as we coach Embassy Suites team members to rise above their job title when the situation calls for it, we also coach (and model) the willingness to do things that might be considered outside our realm of responsibility. From the first day in the hospitality industry, most of us were taught to stop and pick up any piece of trash or litter we passed in the hallway. To this day, I can't walk past a scrap of paper on the floor without leaning over to grab it – even when I'm not working.

One of the reasons for that is that no one enters this business as a boss. You literally do it all. If you're a real hotelier and have the heart of hospitality, you never reach the point where something is not your job. It's probably never stopped being your job. Those experiences build on one another over time. The longer you've been in this business, the more natural it becomes – and the more confident you'll be in reacting to whatever may come your way.

Regardless of your position, your job is really to take care of the guest and exceed their expectations. You're not an engineer, a Guest Services Manager or a Director of Sales. You're a hospitality professional, and that means your job is much more than your job description. Your job is our whole business purpose.

So much goes on inside a hotel that there's no shortage of ways to pitch in. And when we all embrace that attitude, it creates engagement in the best possible way. It creates engagement that's based on trust and communication. And once you have that type of culture in place in your hotel, it's something that's likely to stick around for some time to come.

Doing it all can mean looking to help in areas that others overlook

For instance, I used to work in a hotel that would get slammed during breakfast (sound familiar?). The GM would call for all hands on deck, and everyone would come down to get things running smoothly. While most of us would start by bussing tables and pouring coffee, one or two of us would head straight to the breakdown station and start processing dishes for the dishwasher. Because no matter how fast our entire staff could clear the tables, it would quickly pile up in the back for the person cleaning them.

In the process, it created an opportunity to engage with more and more of our fellow team members. It elevated the spirit of teamwork because everyone saw we were not only serving the guests, we were supporting each other.

At the same time, we were building trust and getting to know more about the people with whom we worked. It created bonds in unexpected ways.

"We all do it all" starts from the top down

If the spirit of everyone doing it all isn't modeled by leadership, it's not going to last. Of course, it is something that any team member can take upon themselves and do on their own. But a great leader really sets the tone for it. Because as much as we'd like to think that we'd go above and beyond no matter the circumstance, more often than not if our extra effort isn't recognized or appreciated, we'll lose interest.

We talk so much about the guest, but the best way to serve the guest is oftentimes to serve each other first. And when we all do it all, we just naturally find more and more ways to contribute.

Always be open minded

No matter how long you've been in this business, every now and then something is going to come up at your hotel that will make you stop and think. Maybe it's a guest request you've never heard before, or a problem you've never seen. Either way, there are times when you are going to have to think outside the box and maybe move outside of your personal comfort zone a little bit.

When that's the case, it's best to turn to your team to find a solution. It's an opportunity to engage with others and show them that you respect and value their contributions. Because as we look to others for guidance, it helps build their confidence in the process.

So when you see something and you're not sure how to react, ask for the advice of one of your fellow team members. Their answer just might be the solution that will help you solve the same problem with ease and grace the next time.

Make it part of your day to explore outside of your department

One of the best ways to grow in your career is to wear many hats. No matter what role you serve, you can always look for ways to lend a helping hand. For instance, maybe once every couple of weeks you could come in 20 minutes early and offer to help someone in a different department. They'll appreciate the help, and you might learn a new side of the business that you really enjoy. Better yet, look for new ways to contribute. Even if it seems small, if it's meaningful to you, it's worth it.

For instance, what if you notice that the fire extinguishers are covered in dust? In fifteen seconds, you could probably wipe all of that dust away. And the truth is, it might go unnoticed. It might never come back around to you. But if we each find little ways to *make a difference* and leave things better than we found them, we'll be amazed by what happens.

For one, our jobs will get easier. With so many people looking for ways to contribute, there's a lot less to worry about. Secondly, it opens our eyes to new possibilities. If you've ever stayed or worked in a poorly kept hotel, you'll know what I'm talking about. Because the more things are wrong or out of place, the harder it is to notice them all – especially the smaller ones. And finally, we find ourselves with more time to serve others. It's an opportunity to excel.

Culture is all of those little things put together. "We all do it all" doesn't just mean the little things. It's leadership and recognition. It's engagement, innovation and appreciation. It's how we feel and act as teams. And when new people join our organization, those are the things they notice right away. They might call it attention to detail, but it's really our culture in its purest form. And it all starts with you.

CHAPTER 8
EVERYONE LOVES APPLAUSE

CHAPTER 8
EVERYONE LOVES APPLAUSE

Applause is something that most people grow up with. As kids, maybe it's our teachers who applaud us for doing a good job on a test or for something as simple as perfect attendance. Hopefully our parents encouraged us at home and applauded our efforts when they saw us trying something new – even if we weren't that good at it. It could even have been during a baseball game, when the stands were packed with parents and fans cheering us on as we gave it our best shot. But as we get older, applause is something that we often start to see less and less of. In fact, we're probably more likely to give applause than receive it.

This provides us with a unique opportunity because at work, we can all give and receive applause openly. And when we do, that spirit of encouragement gives people the confidence they need to reach new heights. Because when we receive applause, it shines the spotlight on us. And while it might embarrass some of us a little at times, it's the good kind of embarrassment. The kind that can make you a little uncomfortable, but in the end puts a smile on your face.

Whether or not giving recognition freely is something that comes naturally to you, very few people are satisfied in their work if they never receive any recognition. And whether we do it publicly in front of the whole team or pull someone aside to give a genuine thank you, we all should make it a priority to stand up and give those around us a round of applause from time to time. The more you do, the more natural it becomes and the better you get at doing it.

So even if you're not someone who naturally gives applause, it's one of those things that we should all strive to do more of. And the best way to break out is just to do it. In fact, if it's your first time in a while, it will probably make a real impression on the person on the other end. It can be even more impactful because of the absence. And like many of the other themes we've discussed in this book, the more that it's practiced in your hotel, the more that team members see it modeled from leadership, the more likely it is to become a permanent pillar of culture in your hotel.

Often when someone is a little uncomfortable giving applause, it's simply because they're out of practice. Some of the discomfort likely comes from the thinking that it has to be something very big. It doesn't. It can come from small and powerful things. Just because it's small doesn't make it any less profound.

So what's the difference between applause and recognition?

For me, applause really implies a group setting. It's recognition given freely in front of a group of our peers. And at Embassy, the best way to do that is often through our Daily Huddles. The person who starts the applause feels great, the person who receives the applause feels great, and best of all, it inspires everyone else in the room. When other team members see it, they'll want to get some of that applause, too!

I've always been a believer that the greatest gifts are the ones you give, not the ones you receive. We grow in so many ways when we are generous in spirit. Generosity is not necessarily about money. You can be generous with your time, your comments and your thoughts. The ideal is being in an environment where you feel comfortable expressing yourself, and the more you can express yourself, the freer you are to celebrate other people.

As we start to applaud others more, we develop an appreciation for the gifts that they bring to the table. The opposite of that is jealousy. And in an environment filled with jealousy, the last thing anyone wants is to have the spotlight turned on them. If that were the atmosphere in your hotel, can you imagine the impact it would have on your team? On the guest experience?

Fortunately, that's not a problem I've seen often with Embassy. Because as a brand, I think we do a great job of recognizing the importance of every individual and try to empower them to do whatever it takes to make the guest experience better.

The benefits of giving applause are twofold

One of the reasons that giving applause openly and often is such a powerful force is that the benefits of this simple yet thoughtful gesture are twofold. So far, we've discussed some of the emotional benefits - the basic human desire that is fulfilled as we give applause. And even though that alone is reason enough to applaud the accomplishments of those around us, the business reason for applause makes just as strong of a case.

Because as we see others carry out those applause-worthy actions – namely, actions that demonstrate being gracious, engaging and caring – we're really just carrying out the spirit of true hospitality on the most basic level. And it all ties back to the guest experience.

If your team members don't find meaning and fulfillment in their work, they can carry out the actions, but it will never be genuine. Because when someone truly enjoys their work, I've often noticed that it appears to be something they do effortlessly. Rather than being stressed out, they're eager and happy. And someone calm and collected – someone who is gracious, engaging and caring – is exactly the person who you want greeting you at the front door, preparing your omelet with a smile or just stopping to answer a question in the hallway.

Our team members can't create a fantastic experience for our guests if they don't have one, too – and applause is one of the ways to get there.

I'd like to add one last thought. If for no other reason, we should give applause because we deserve it. I can't count the number of times that I've seen people make personal sacrifices in this business, whether it's staying late or filling in for someone else. We work hard, and all of that hard work can't go unnoticed. Embassy has done so much to be proud of, but none of that would have ever come to life without the people who carried it out.

The complimentary cooked-to-order breakfast. The Evening Manager's Reception. The fact that we carry those things out with excellence every single day – on top of everything else we do – is simply amazing. And to see people come into work, put their problems to the side and tackle their duties with a smile on their faces is something from which we can all take pride and inspiration.

CHAPTER 9
PUTTING YOURSELF IN THE GUEST'S SHOES

CHAPTER 9
PUTTING YOURSELF IN THE GUEST'S SHOES

n our business, empathy is the path to success. We need to foster the ability to feel what another is feeling, to imagine ourselves in their predicament, to understand what a big deal a small thing can sometimes be.

I often speak of empathy in terms of imagining the Embassy guest as a guest in your own home. How do you treat a close friend or family member staying with you for a few days? For one thing, you take ownership of their experience. You want them to have a great stay and you will do whatever it takes to make that happen.

Oftentimes the best ways to approach a guest situation is to put yourself in the guest's shoes. When we take a step back – when we remove ourselves from the situation – it's often much easier to see where we can help. But no matter how much we train our team members, no matter how much we try to create a culture that supports true hospitality, it's all for naught if we don't internalize it. A little intuition goes a long way when it comes to making a meaningful connection with our guests.

Here's an example: We pride ourselves at Embassy as being a brand for self-sufficient travelers. That group typically has a very different set of needs and expectations than other groups of travelers. But if we approached each individual guest as if he or she were a seasoned business traveler, we'd miss the mark for a lot of other guests. After all, we're also known to many for our family-friendly environment.

That's where intuition comes in. And to be honest, it's something that takes time and skill. It's the art of hospitality. In just a moment's time, we're often tasked with identifying someone's needs and what it will take to exceed their expectations. The more we do it, the more natural it becomes.

That's why we all need to step back and put ourselves in the guests' shoes from time to time. If we don't, it's a lot like spraying air freshener in a room to mask an odor. We can make things better. It may even seem as if the issue has gone away. But we're not getting to the heart of the matter, which means we're ultimately not solving the problem.

That's because there are two parts to every problem. There's the problem itself – maybe it's a leaky faucet or a broken television – and then there's the situation around the problem. And if we "fix" the problem without addressing the situation it created, it often leaves the person on the other end feeling less than satisfied.

Let's say you go out to dinner with friends to the new restaurant in town that's getting all the rave reviews. When it comes time to order, you decide to try the lamb chops, just like your server recommended. The rest of the table orders, and you enjoy an appetizer before the main course arrives. Everything comes out without a hitch, but there's one problem – your lamb chops somehow came out as pork chops.

Mistakes happen. So you let your server know and he quickly apologizes and promises to return with your entrée. But the fact of the matter is, now everyone has their food except for you. It creates an awkwardness at the table. "I'm starving. Can I start without him?" the other guests might think. So while the first problem might have been solved, it's created a separate problem.

Here's where the real opportunity lies. Perhaps the server offers to bring out a dessert, compliments of the chef. Or maybe the restaurant's general manager visits the table, genuinely expresses his gratitude for your patronage and apologizes for the mistake. Now, we see a completely different situation. Things went wrong, but they didn't stay that way because of that personal interaction. Most people will respond very positively when they're made to feel special and appreciated.

If we can do that with our guests at Embassy, we've won. Mistakes are inevitable, but responding in a compassionate and caring way is what separates Embassy from the rest of the pack.

There's no real substitute for seeing a hotel as the guest does
One very old school approach is to have each new team member spend a night in the hotel so that they can experience the services. Let them see and experience it all, from the

Evening Manager's Reception followed by dinner in the restaurant to a complimentary cooked-to-order breakfast the following morning.

When I first started my career in hospitality, it was often mandatory for people to spend the night and experience the hotel as a guest. And while some hotels still do this, it's unfortunately something that we see less and less of. If this isn't a common practice in your hotel, I recommend you give it a chance. You just might be pleasantly surprised by how much it sticks with people.

What if you and the guest are polar opposites?

Some guests are more demanding than others. Our job is still to make their stay with us the best it can be. We need to be thinking, "How can I help?" and "What can I do?" and then go the extra mile to make it right for the guest.

If I had a roommate, for instance, who invited a guest to stay overnight in our house, whether I like that guest or not doesn't matter. I'm still going to be a gracious host, to pour their coffee in the morning, to ask how they slept. It has nothing to do with my relationship with that person. It's hospitality, pure and simple.

Putting yourself in the guest's shoes can be a delicate dance. We are a people business, but ultimately, we are still a business.

We're there to serve, but there is a line. You can be gracious, engaging and caring while also being a responsible steward of your business.

We don't communicate to our team members that the guest is right and whatever happened is wrong. What we're communicating is that it's not important who is right or who is wrong. What's important is that the guest feels happy and satisfied. And in doing so, you're being true to the brand and the people you work with.

CHAPTER 10
WHAT'S BETTER THAN SOLVING
A PROBLEM?
AVOIDING IT IN THE FIRST PLACE

CHAPTER 10
WHAT'S BETTER THAN SOLVING A PROBLEM?
AVOIDING IT IN THE FIRST PLACE

P roblem resolution is a topic that comes up often in the hospitality industry. When something goes wrong for a guest, what can we do to make things right? The trick is, we can't do just enough to make it okay. We have to make a gesture that is grand enough to truly overcome the negative experience.

Yet the real magic lies in avoiding problems in the first place. The more we can avoid problems before they arise, the more we can offer a consistently great guest experience. The more we can deliver a great guest experience, the more loyalty we'll build. And the quiet joy that comes from knowing that you're doing all that you can to avoid problems far surpasses the simple appreciation you get from making something right that shouldn't have ever been wrong.

The problem with problem resolution
In the hospitality industry, we consider it a given that problems are inevitable. That makes sense. We are human, and so are our guests. Another classic adage in our business is that you can create more customer loyalty if you fix a problem than if you never had the problem in the first place. Sometimes that's true.

Our culture at Embassy Suites supports fixing problems. Our team members all know about the 100% Satisfaction Guarantee and that each one of them is empowered to make it right for any guest with a problem.

Our GMs reinforce that idea and urge their teams to solve any problems their guests may have. But in our current economy, few GMs can really afford to give away their rooms for free, at least not often.

So what happens is that we engage in a sort of bidding war with the unhappy guest. We're thinking, "What will it take to make it up to you?" Maybe we start with microwave popcorn. If that doesn't seem to do it, then we might offer a complimentary in-room movie or a free dessert in the hotel restaurant. No matter what we do, the end result is that we still stepped on that guest's foot.

Last year, our SALT scores indicated that 25% of our guests had a problem with their last stay. Out of that group – the quarter of our guests who say something went wrong – only 27% of them say the problem was resolved by meeting or exceeding their expectations. For those people in that select group, we succeeded. We can hope they walked away feeling more loyalty to Embassy than they had before the problem.

As I said, the trick to problem resolution is that we can't do just enough to make it okay. We have to make a gesture grand enough to truly overcome the negative experience.

One of the best parts of our culture is that we give our team members the opportunity to make our guests happy. When it works, when we're able to offer a terrific solution to the problem, to do something that not only solves the problem but makes someone's day, then that is one really great feeling.

The more we can engage our team members in our culture of **Make a Difference**, the more we can offer a consistently great guest experience across the brand. The more we can deliver a great guest experience, the more loyalty we'll build. And in the process, we'll start to see fewer and fewer problems.

When it comes right down to it, problem resolution isn't a tactical topic. It's a cultural issue. When our GMs are building our culture – when they're talking with team members about how they see themselves *making a difference*, when they're asking how they think gracious, engaging and caring might apply to running either the front desk or a vacuum cleaner – then they're actually building better guest experiences.

Don't forget to listen

Circle of Leadership GM Terry Crawford of Embassy Suites Charlotte – Concord/Golf Resort & Spa says that a problem stays a problem without any interaction. Listening is the most important part of interacting with someone, although people don't usually associate listening as interaction because it's not physical activity. In your eagerness to get something done, it's easy to skip over the seemingly passive act of listening. Solving a problem takes focus, and if you don't know what the problem is, then you can't solve it. It sounds elementary, I know, but it's also brilliant in its simplicity.

Whether it's intentional or not, when we don't listen, it often leads to taking the easy way out. That makes any problem twice the size it was to begin with. The worst thing we can do is talk ourselves into a shortcut like, "Let's just do a quick fix" or, "I can let this one slide." By avoiding that, we approach problem solving on a much higher level.

For one thing, it allows us to think more long-term, which means our solutions are more impactful. It gives us a chance to gather more information and think through various outcomes before putting our solution into effect. I don't think any of us take the easy way out because of ill intent. Occasionally, we find ourselves in a time-crunch and feel pressured to check things off the list.

The important thing to keep in mind is that **Make a Difference** isn't a band-aid sort of hospitality. It's a holistic, long-term point of view.

So how can we overcome those obstacles and become better at problem resolution?

For me, it really comes down to two things. The first is ownership. If you're the first to see a problem, it's your problem. And the reality is, it might be something that you can't personally fix. If a guest stops me in the hallway because the remote control in their room isn't working, the only thing I'd know how to do would be to check the batteries. If it's not that, I'm fresh out of solutions.

But just because I'm not the one who can provide the fix doesn't mean that I can't take ownership over the situation. I can find an engineer and ask for their help in solving the problem. I can follow up with the guest and make sure everything is okay. That simple gesture is often enough to make our guests feel appreciated. And if for some reason the problem still hasn't been fixed, 10 times out of 10 I'd like to know. Because those unsolved problems are a pet peeve of mind. It's a missed opportunity, and one that should never have been missed.

The second is transparency. It's being able to talk openly and honestly about the problems that we see in our hotels, without hurting anyone's feelings. If you've ever been hit by something too hard on the nose, you'll know what I'm talking about. Your eyes swell up and they start to water. Your only focus is on the pain in your nose, even if it's only for a moment.

But that's the same reaction you'll find if you try to address a problem by attacking or shifting the blame on an individual. So how do you say it so the person on the other end can hear you, and without hurting anyone's feelings?

The key to giving genuine, constructive criticism is that you have to have respect for the other person's style. Before you give any sort of criticism, make sure that it's something important and that it has an actionable result. I would never want to give anyone criticism, constructive or otherwise, if it's a very small and insignificant thing. We all have bigger things to worry about, and giving criticism where it isn't needed can undermine your efforts to give true constructive criticism when it counts.

The hard part about giving criticism is that you have to be completely honest. You have to say exactly what you mean without minimizing or dramatizing it. The best approach is simply to be as factual and as specific as possible. I have a friend who uses an approach that she calls the "criticism sandwich." First, you talk about something the other person is doing well. Then you offer the criticism. And finally, you top it off with another compliment.

You might first talk about one of the person's strengths, and how valuable it is to the team. Then, calmly and unemotionally, discuss the issue at hand. Finish up by once again praising the person's strengths and expressing your confidence that he or she can overcome this one issue. It sort of bridges the trust and lets the person know that you are not trying to tear them down or apart.

Everything you say must be true, though. If you praise others for things you don't believe they're really much good at, you'll undermine their ability to trust your feedback, whether it's negative or positive.

In a lot of ways, constructive criticism is like having a mirror held up to you. When we look in the mirror, we're looking to see that our hair is combed, that there's nothing caught between our teeth. We're looking for a true reflection and an opportunity to get better. It's a tremendous gift for anybody who is open to receive feedback about themselves, and mastering the skill can help you have more meaningful conversations with your team.

More than anything else, culture shapes problem resolution

As individual hotels, our approaches to problem resolution are a direct reflection of our culture. If you put the right kind of culture in place in your hotel, you'll find that problem resolution suddenly becomes much less of a problem.

CHAPTER 11
MODELING LEADERSHIP
STARTS WITH YOU

95

MODELING LEADERSHIP STARTS WITH YOU

When I think about leadership, the first person who comes to mind is Martin Luther King, Jr. He was firm in his beliefs and inspirational in his message at a time of drastic change in history. Another great example is Mahatma Gandhi. During the Indian independence movement, he became the face of a nation by fighting oppression with kindness.

So what do those two men – along with countless other great leaders – have in common? They inspired others. They inspired them in a way that built trust, and in doing so were able to achieve things far greater than themselves. Through that inspiration, their leadership lives on.

So how can we inspire those around us? How can we become better leaders? It starts with thinking about leadership and understanding some of those traits that make up a great leader. From there, the path to leadership will be as individual as the person behind it. When you find something that you're passionate about, oftentimes you'll naturally find yourself becoming a leader in the process.

What's at the heart of a great leader?
Being a good leader is simple, but that doesn't mean it's easy.

It can mean doing what's right instead of taking the easy way out. It's being passionate and looking at the big picture. It's being inclusive and transparent. It's truly embodying our **Make a Difference** culture and helping those around us grow.

Great leadership means putting your ego to the side and doing what needs to be done. It has nothing to do with your job title. A true leader won't hesitate to pick up a piece of trash on the floor or answer a ringing phone. And while those may seem like small gestures, what that leader is really doing is setting the example. They're inspiring others. When you can do that, you leave behind a legacy.

A common misconception I see is that people think leadership is simply meant for the executive leadership team. And while the executive team is certainly charged with communicating the company vision and steering the ship, true leadership can be found at all levels of an organization.

Leadership doesn't have to mean that you're in charge of managing a group of people. It's taking a sense of ownership over what you can control and inspiring those around you. As stated earlier, I like to say that the 'E' in our Embassy Suites logo stands for "everybody does everything" – and that includes leading.

By being a leader, by being a good steward of what you are responsible for, you are able to elevate the stature of the organization. You're able to elevate the stature of your team, and most importantly, you're able to elevate yourself. Leadership doesn't stop with you – you're where it begins.

So how can we make that leap? By building relationships. By asking those around us what's important and meaningful to them and helping them get there. Just as we teach our team members to do whatever it takes to serve our guests and exceed their expectations, the best leaders extend that same hospitality to their teams.

Sometimes the most important skill of leadership is being able to assemble a team that is stronger than the sum of its parts. Those leaders have a vision, but from there, they are able to pull together a team of individuals who can turn that vision into action. Rather than doing the heavy lifting, they're able to plant the seed for an idea and let their team grow it.

Leadership means taking ownership

Like many people, one of my first real experiences with leadership came to me by sheer accident. In 1999, the GM of the hotel that I was working for at the time saw that other hotels had websites. Not wanting to fall behind the competition, he decided that we needed a website. And although I didn't know any more about launching a website than anyone else, I was charged with the task.

Even though I didn't know the first thing about web development, I started by simply looking at the websites of other local hotels. Once I started to get a feel for what a good website looked like, I reached out to someone who's site I admired. I met with him over coffee, and he taught me the very basics of internet marketing. Eventually, I started linking my new hotel website to other travel related sites. I made a point to look for new sites every week, and I kept an updated spreadsheet of all those different links, which I shared with other Embassy DOSs monthly. The list kept growing, as did the distribution, and eventually it caught the attention of someone in the corporate office.

In a short amount of time, I started being known as an expert – even though I felt far from it. That simple act would end up being the thing that got my foot in the door by starting to receive recognition from and build relationships with the corporate team – and it started with taking ownership over a task.

A trait that I admire most among great leaders is that they're not self-serving. A true leader isn't simply telling people what to do; a true leader helps people reach their full potential. The beautiful thing is that this style of powerful leadership tends to create a ripple effect – people tend to perform at their highest when they work for someone who inspires them. They are also able to witness firsthand what inspirational leadership is really like.

In my experience, I've seen that leadership is equal parts experience and intuition – and the two are closely intertwined.

Every day, we're learning new things and growing our base of experiences. But part of what makes leadership special is that it comes from the inside, too. When that experience combines with intuition, it's spontaneous and genuine.

Leadership through service

True leaders know that their success depends on the success of their teams. I'm often surprised by just how humble these leaders are, especially when you consider all of their achievements. A true leader is able to rally his or her team around a cause, to give people the confidence and encouragement they need to tackle new challenges with enthusiasm. The result is an inspired and engaged team of people who enjoy and take pride in their work.

Today, I often hear the term "service leadership." It can be applied to practically any industry, but for me it particularly rings true in hospitality. It's a very basic fundamental frame of mind with which to approach leadership. Service leadership is about serving people's most basic needs, cutting away the clutter of everything else. It's not necessarily a matter of doing things more efficiently or more effectively. It's about doing them better.

Humble leaders possess a careful mix of humility and pride. You'll often notice when a humble leader receives praise, they'll quickly mention the help and support they received from their team. Another big thing is transparency. A true leader doesn't say one thing and mean another. They're genuine, open and honest.

Becoming a leader starts today

Find something in your hotel that is meaningful to you and assign yourself responsibility over that area. Maybe it's your hotel's **Make a Difference** committee, or maybe it's finding a better way of doing something that's always bugged you. If you find yourself stuck and don't know where to turn next, reach out to someone else. They might just give you the nudge you need to make everything come together.

CHAPTER 12
INSPIRING EMPLOYEES GOES FAR BEYOND THE WORKPLACE

105

CHAPTER 12

INSPIRING EMPLOYEES GOES FAR BEYOND THE WORKPLACE

Employee engagement is most impactful when it starts to spill over outside of the workplace. In our business, it's something we see often. The truth is, it's hard to "act" a certain way at work if that's not who you really are. For many people in hospitality, myself included, it's second nature to pick up a piece of trash on the floor. It's natural to greet someone when they enter a room and to be a good host. In fact, that's the sweet spot for employee engagement: Creating an environment where employees become all stars just by being themselves.

You see, our **Make a Difference** culture starts with the brand, and it's expressed by our team members and with our guests. But it's most impactful when it extends beyond the four walls of your hotel. And at its finest, culture is something that people take home with them, sharing it with their families and their communities.

Fortunately, that's something that I see happening all the time. And truth be told, when you truly embrace the values of being gracious, engaging and caring, it's only natural that it will stick with you – even after you clock out at the end of the day.

For an example, look no further than the I Can Make a Difference Award. We received an incredible response to the program and had many nominations, in part because we were inviting people to share what's important to them outside of work. People shared what projects they're involved with in their communities, what they're passionate about and what it would mean if they had some additional money to work towards that goal.

The winners took home a prize of $5,000 to be used in support of the projects of their choosing. And what impressed me, although perhaps it was to be expected, is that all of the nominees talked about serving others, about *making a difference* in their local communities.

Greg Riley can Make a Difference

One of the winners, Greg Riley of Embassy Suites Los Angeles – International Airport/South, told me how he received his package in the mail with a video camera and other tools for sharing his story. He told me how he took that package home and shared it with his family.

His son told him, "Dad, at this point, it doesn't matter if you win or not. You've already done something good, and whatever happens, it's going to be better for everybody."

It was really a touching moment, and it truly illustrates the point. It's a perfect integration of his work and home lives. It was touching because he brought his work home with him to share with his family, but also because he brought his personal passion to work with him and shared it so openly. At that point, there's no line between personal and professional. He's integrated and complete, and his family and coworkers both have the pleasure of knowing Greg on a personal and genuine level.

Modeling **Make a Difference** *can be expressed through the simplest of gestures*

All of us find ways to be gracious, engaging and caring outside of work, even if we don't take the time to recognize that we're doing it.

When you stop and take the time to give directions to an out-of-town driver who's lost in your city, you're *making a difference*.

When you return your grocery cart, and then take a few extra steps to return another cart that someone else left in the parking lot, you're *making a difference*.

When you're driving and you pause for a moment to let someone out in traffic, you're *making a difference*.

Or when you volunteer your time with an organization that is meaningful to you, you're *making a difference*.

There are countless ways that we can all *make a difference*, but in the end, it comes down to leaving things better than you found them. When you do that, you'll finish every day with a feeling of pride – in the fact that you gave it your all, and that you gave it your best effort.

A friend once told me that when you leave work at the end of the day, you should feel as if you'd be proud to put your initials by everything you did that day. For a Guest Services Manager, that could mean that you greeted every guest with a smile and showed true hospitality. And you stand behind what you've done.

For an engineer, maybe it means you quickly solved a few of the problems you've seen before, and even fixed a thing or two that you noticed and made better without being told to do so, simply because it was meaningful to you.

And if you're a General Manager, that might mean that you made a connection with everyone in your hotel. That you did your best to deliver a great experience for everyone who walked through your doors, and that you took the time to have meaningful and personal interactions with your team members.

When we do those things, we're proud of what we do, and it builds trust and respect among our teams. When we do them every day, it's called leadership.

What really matters to people?

At the end of the day, I think that what matters most to people is communication. People want to have a voice. They want to feel that their opinions are heard and respected. It creates a connectedness, and just like Greg Riley, it blurs the line between people's work and personal lives.

And those individuals, at least in my experience, happen to be the most helpful and genuine people on your team. They're people you can trust to handle any situation, because you know that the solution they come up with will come from a genuinely good place.

It gives them an opportunity to take what's meaningful and important to them and share it with others. To take their unique skills, their personal flair, and apply it to their everyday work.

It creates strong teams. It creates world-class guest experiences. And ultimately, it leads to happy team members who find meaning in their work. And in my book, that's the makings of an all-star team.